TOUCHING

AURAS

Touching Auras

The Aura of a Baby

Aislin

Table of Contents

Introduction 1
The Aura of a Baby 4
The Needs of a Baby 6
Seeing the Aura 8
Interpreting the Aura 10
Touching Auras 13
Conclusion 16

Introduction

Babies are precious things. They are sweet, delicate, and have a natural vulnerability that rouses the protective instincts of most adults. And with the arrival of a baby comes the fun of buying all the cute little baby things that fill stores around the globe. The home that houses a newborn can be filled with joy. In truth, babies are more than precious; they are magickal.

But babies aren't all fun and games. In fact, many parents are downright miserable at some point during baby's first year. There are diapers to be changed, you don't get any sleep, and sometimes nothing you do will make your precious little angel stop screaming. That's just the reality of being a parent. It's not always fun, even when you love your children more than life itself.

As parents, we have tools to protect and teach our children. Some of these tools are instinct. Others are things we pick up along the way, often after making far too many mistakes. One of the tools we come equipped with is our own natural energy. Babies can sense it, especially the energy of the mother. Mother and child were bound together for nine months, after all. While babies can also recognize the energies of the father and sometimes even siblings, the energy of the mother is more familiar. This energy, especially the energy of the ever-present aura, can be used in a positive way to influence your baby. Older children can also benefit from these techniques, but they're really designed to comfort and relax infants under a year old.

The purpose of this book is to learn to use your aura to help your child. This is a simple process, but it can take time to learn. I know it took a great deal of time for me to master. At the time of this writing, I have two young sons, ages five and seven years. My oldest child, Griffin, was the dream baby. He never needed me to calm him. He ate, he slept, he smiled, he played. Not all babies are like that. My youngest, Falcon, was a colicky baby. He couldn't help it, of course, but he cried almost constantly, or so it seemed. I had to come up with something other than bouncing little Falcon on my knee, for his sake and for my own.

Falcon, as it turned out, was a special needs baby. He was always upset, always hypersensitive, and he couldn't stand to have people looking at him. The only thing he did well was eat, provided no one touched him, talked to him, or looked at him while he was eating. This is a bigger problem than you might think, especially with an infant. Despite all the help I sought, there didn't seem to be much either I or the doctors could do. Even the child development specialists were at a loss. We all tried our best, but nothing seemed to calm little Falcon.

At that point, I'd been a practicing Wiccan for most of my life and a High Priestess for a couple years. I remember thinking to myself, "Surely I have a tool to help me here. I've got a tool for everything else." After some consideration, I realized I did indeed have a tool, one that every creature on this earth shared. I had an aura. If I could use that aura to calm an aggressive dog, as I had often done in the past, surely I could use it to soothe my upset baby.

As it turned out, I could. Since a baby is not a dog, it took a little practice on my part. But it wasn't long before I was able to help Falcon sleep. Not only that, but with this technique Falcon was able to endure eye contact and even consented to being held by someone other than me. Five years later, I still use my own aura to help Falcon through difficult situations, especially those involving strangers. And now he's starting to do it for himself, and that is rewarding and necessary, since he started school this year.

But don't think Falcon is the only child I used it on. Once I discovered it worked, I found myself able to help Griffin concentrate, which has always been a challenge for him. My children began to truly blossom and show their potential. Even better, my bond with them was strengthened, and I didn't think that was possible.

Your aura is a powerful tool, one you can use to soothe the babies in your life. You may have a son or daughter, niece or nephew, or another baby in your family. All of these children can benefit from the energy of your own aura. All you need is patience and practice.

The Aura of a Baby

An unborn fetus is full of potential. It carries within it the ability to hear, see, touch, taste, and smell. This is true even when these abilities have not yet developed. The fact that they *will* develop is the beautiful part of it all. A fetus cannot yet experience life or make human connections outside of the enveloping security of the mother, but these things will come. The fetus will one day take a breath, will open its eyes, and even smile at a familiar face. Maybe it can't yet, but these things will happen. An unborn fetus also carries within it the potential to develop its own electrical field, a field referred to as the aura.

As soon as it is born a baby becomes more than a collection of cells and a series of fascinating developmental stages. When the baby draws its first breath it exhibits its own personality and begins to interact with the world. It is also at this moment that the baby begins to shine with the first signs of an aura. Having been present at many births, especially the births of Pagan children, I have seen this happen for myself. The child emerges into the world, takes a deep breath, gets ready to scream, and begins to glow with the palest of auras. I've also seen what happens when a child comes into the world not breathing. In those terrifying moments when doctors or midwives are trying to get the infant to breathe, there is no glow. Not until the child actually takes his or her first breath does the aura make its presence known.

All of this has led me to firmly believe that the aura is composed of a combination of matter and radiation. This auric mix is drawn into the body and absorbed by the living tissue of the child. Once fully absorbed, it begins to radiate outward. It is only barely noticeable because it's very thin. So thin that you have to be looking closely to notice it at all. But if you do look closely, and if you have some experience with seeing auras, you'll eventually see it. It can certainly be felt, especially in very young children. It is no coincidence that we are drawn to babies. Their auras are clear and pure, and we all instinctively want a little bit of that purity for ourselves.

At first, the aura of a baby is colorless. They haven't formed a strong enough personality to affect its color. But slowly, as the energy of the aura attracts and absorbs particles and energy from the atmosphere, it begins to glow a faint silver-blue color. Sometimes this color is more silver than blue, but it's rarely another color before the child reaches one year of age.

At approximately the one year mark, when the intelligence of the mind begins to form, the aura will begin to take on its own color. The color can be affected by personality or the environment as experienced during the first year. There's not a lot you can do about the innate personality of your baby, but you can do something about the environment. Make sure your baby is outside as much as possible during their first year of life. Go to the park, the zoo, or just for a long walk. The more nature your baby experiences the better, but even a walk through a city is better than being cooped up in the house all day. The aura of a baby who has experienced nature is almost always brighter and healthier than that of a baby who has spent most of its first year confined to the house. So get outside; your baby's aura will be healthier for it.

Society has trained us not to see auras, even the pure and sweet auras of babies. Seeing the aura of your child might be fun, but it is not strictly necessary when touching and influencing the aura of your baby. Babies, remember, all have a silvery-blue aura, though the exact shade may differ a little. Because the auras are basically the same through the first year of life, you can work with your child's aura without actually being able to see it.

The Needs of a Baby

We all know about the very basic needs of a child because they don't differ that much from the basic needs of adults. Food, water, shelter, sleep. But children also need love and security, especially babies. Many studies have shown that babies who are not held and nurtured in their first few days of life often suffer health problems directly linked to this lack of touch. They can develop a failure to thrive, a condition often connected to large orphanages where children have all their physical needs met but are not given the security and love they need. In the case of newborns, the denial of physical contact can, in some cases, actually lead to death.

It is a given fact that all children need this love and security in order to thrive, both physically and spiritually. In our circle, we like to say that children need "perfect love and perfect trust". How do we give this to our babies? By responding to their needs. An infant cannot be greedy. An infant cannot ask for something he does not need. An infant cannot plot to manipulate you. They simply exist, and they have needs that must be met. Since they cannot meet their own needs, we have to take on that responsibility.

One of the first things I realized when my oldest son was born was that I was his only security. As a parent, as his parent, he would initially take his cues only from me. How I treated him, how I responded to him, would dictate the kind of person he would turn out to be. We've all heard someone say we should just let babies cry it out. I was even criticized for not allowing either of my children to do so. One woman told me she let her baby cry for six hours. Hours! This baby, by the way, was only four weeks old. A baby isn't born with the knowledge to soothe and calm himself.

If we don't teach him how to comfort himself, how is he supposed to learn?

An infant's entire world revolves around comfort and discomfort. If something is wrong, if something is uncomfortable, babies cry. If everything is right with the world, babies don't cry. Sometimes it can seem to us as if babies are crying for no reason, but this just isn't true. We don't always know what's wrong, and when we do we can't always fix it, but we can let our children know we're there. It's either that or put a crying infant in the crib to cry himself into an exhausted sleep, and I just could never do that. I know I wouldn't want to be left alone in my room if I was crying myself sick even as an adult, so why would I inflict that on my baby? We're there for our friends when they need us, even if there's nothing in particular we can do. Being there for a baby should be much more important, even if we can't fix the problem.

You might be wondering why all this matters in an e-book about the aura of a baby. Earlier I said there wasn't a lot that can be done to influence the innate personality of your baby. That's true, but only to a certain extent. You can't change the nature of your baby, but you can let your baby know you are there for him. Not by using words, but by using actions. This means lots of cuddling, touching, talking, and singing. It also means feeding on demand (while making sure your child is getting enough to eat) and changing diapers as soon as they need changing. Doing all these things will give your baby a sense of love and security, a sense of perfect love and perfect trust. This will brighten and strengthen the aura without you ever needing to do anything mystical with your child.

Of course, if you do want to do something mystical with your child…

Seeing the Aura

Reading an aura, whether that of an adult or a child, isn't all that hard, but it does take practice. Before you can read the aura, you must be able to see it. If you aren't very good as seeing auras, or if you've never seen any auras before, you'll want to start with yourself. Your hand, to be specific. Once you can see the aura around your own hand, you can move on to other things. But for now, just worry about seeing the aura shining around your hand.

Before you begin, you'll need the right lighting. The harsh lighting of most homes won't do it. Soft light, like a low wattage lamp, is better if you want to see some results early on. If the light is too bright, consider tossing a white cloth over top. As long as it's not a fire hazard, this can help soften the light. If it is a fire hazard, come up with a different plan. I know, I shouldn't have to say that, but I find if it goes unsaid, someone starts a fire entirely by accident.

Find yourself a large piece of white paper. It should be large enough to place your whole hand on, but even larger is better. You can even use a bed sheet as long as it's white. A white couch would also do the trick. The important thing is that you'll be able to place your hand on a white background. At home, I have a large sheet I use to teach the art of seeing the aura.

Place your dominant hand (right hand for those who are right-handed) on the white background with your fingers splayed and relax your eyes. Let them blur a bit and blink when you need to; dry eyes have a hard time seeing the glow of an aura. Don't stare directly as your hand. Instead, let your gaze play about the areas immediately surrounding your hand, especially between the fingers. Here your aura will overlap, making it easier to see.

TOUGHING AURAS

After a while, if you are patient enough and relaxed enough, you will begin to see a soft haze around your hand. If you continue to practice, you will eventually start noticing colors. Beginners usually only see a single color, but with practice you will be able to see all the colors of the aura. But this takes time and practice, so don't expect to see a rainbow of colors on your first try. It's extremely rare for a beginner to enjoy success so early on.

Don't get discouraged if you see absolutely nothing the first few times. This is normal. It takes practice to become good at anything, including see auras. It might seem hard at first, but with time and practice seeing auras can become almost second nature. It's kind of like reading a book. Before you learn to read, it's just a jumble on a page. But once you've learned to read, the words come together and you can barely imagine not being able to make sense of them.

Once you've learned to see your own aura, practice with other people. I like to use pets. If you can get your dog or cat to sit still on a white bed sheet, you can practice without too much difficulty. You can also practice using your own baby, especially if the sheets in the crib are white. Just lay the baby down for a nap and practice away. If your child is under a year, don't expect to see anything other than a silver or blue haze.

Practice with anything and everything. Even inanimate objects have auras. You can try rocks, books, or even baby toys. That teddy bear has its own aura, though it will be dimmer than the aura of a human or animal.

Interpreting the Aura

Once you can see the many colors of the aura, you have to know what the colors mean. The aura can be any color, or any combination of colors. You might see stripes, layers, spots, or flares of different colors. What the different configurations mean is generally something you'll have to determine for yourself, but the colors do have specific meanings.

White — Some colors are rarer than others. Such is the case with white. It is common to see white when you are first learning to see auras, but once you can see the actual colors, you'll notice white is very rare indeed. When an aura is actually white (as opposed to appearing white) it indicates purity and truth. White sparkles show up when someone is speaking the unvarnished truth.

Red — This color represents strength, will, and strong passions. A dark red may indicate a person who has a quick temper or is impulsive. All reds indicate some nervous tendencies. Accompanying colors may explain how this nervous energy is utilized.

Pink — It should come as no surprise that this is the color of love. Pink shows up when someone is experiencing intense feelings of love. It can also represent pure compassion or a love of art and beauty. Murkier shades of pink often indicate someone who is immature for his or her age.

Orange — Creativity, thoughtfulness, and warmth are generally represented by an orange aura. A dirty orange may indicate a person who is prideful or full of vanity. Lighter oranges usually mean that person has a great deal of self-control. If you see orange spots, these may indicate kidney problems.

Yellow — Usually representing optimism and intense mental activity, yellow can also indicate wisdom and the willingness to learn. Dirty yellows can mean the owner is intensely shy. Bright yellow spots usually mean that person takes good physical care of him or herself.

Green — Sympathy and calmness are revealed by the color green. Someone with a lot of green in their aura is generally reliable and may be talented in the healing arts. Dirty greens usually indicate someone who is jealous or uncertain.

Blue — This color indicates inner peace and serenity. Almost all blues are positive, but the best shade is a deep royal blue. Royal blue almost always appears in the aura of someone who has found his or her purpose in life. This could be work related, but it doesn't have to be. Blue is also an intensely spiritual color; whiter blues often indicate someone who has found their spiritual path. Dirty or murky blues usually mean someone who is depressed or incredibly moody.

Indigo — People with this color can generally handle whatever life throws at them. These people are worldly, practical, and ready for anything.

Violet — The color of questing, violet indicates someone who is seeking something in life. Dirty shades usually indicate someone who has obstacles to overcome. This person may also be feeling misunderstood.

Brown — Auras of this shade are usually confined to people who exhibit 'earthy' tendencies. Perhaps this is someone who is establishing new roots; homebuyers often have brown auras. This color may also indicate someone who is centered and stable. Black spots within the brown usually represent a state of flux.

Black — If there is a color of protection, it is black. Black is a commonly used color when it comes to spells and rituals, but this isn't a good color to have as an aura. It often indicates the person is hiding something, usually to their own detriment. Spots of black often indicate spiritual imbalances or physical ailments.

Silver Lights — Silver rarely shows up as a color on its own, but silver lights are common. Often they are interpreted to mean pregnancy, but this isn't always the case. If it is, my seven-year-old son is pregnant! No, silver lights indicate a period of great creativity. Someone who is producing a creative work will almost always have silver lights dancing through his or her aura. Pregnancy is one of the 'creative works' silver lights may indicate, but it's far from the only one.

Most of the colors of the aura are a combination of those indicated here. Each color, regardless of where it appears in the aura, has a meaning and should not be dismissed, not even in an infant. Remember, however, that most infants will have an aura of silvery-blue. It will take time for the true colors of the aura to reveal themselves, but it will eventually happen.

Touching Auras

So we've talked about the needs of a baby and the details of a baby's aura. We've discussed seeing and interpreting the aura of both adults and babies. But how do we, as parents, use this knowledge to benefit an infant? We can't tell them to go to their rooms and calm themselves with exercises we might recommend to an adult or even an older child. Instead, we have to take the lead and use our own aura as a guide.

I was lucky with my first born. Griffin was a calm child who slept well and rarely cried. I never really understood the mothers who were exhausted all the time. I slept well enough and my baby was full of fun and joy. What was wrong with all the mothers out there?

When Falcon was born, I figured out exactly what was wrong with them. They were exhausted *all* of the time. They rarely got to sleep more than an hour in a row and some of their babies were colicky. My own baby was colicky and refused to sleep for more than forty-five minutes, even when I was holding him. Exhaustion doesn't begin to describe it.

Still, I figured anyone could handle being sleep deprived for a few weeks. But when Falcon turned four months old and still wasn't sleeping, I knew it was time to put my own knowledge to work. I started projecting calm energy into his aura as I held him, helping him fall asleep. Once I'd put him in his crib, I was able to project through the bedroom door, helping him stay asleep or even sooth himself back to sleep. It worked, and I was able to sleep four hours in a row for the first time in months.

The method I used is effective with all children, but it's most effective with infants. If you can't yet see your own aura, or that of your baby, you can keep practicing. But you don't need to see the aura to work with it. You can visualize your aura touching your baby's, giving your child comfort, security, trust, and love. You can calm your baby, or help him figure out a problem, simply by projecting the right color into your baby's aura.

Doing this is as simple as breathing. Actually, breathing is a great way to begin the visualization. Choose your color and see it as smoke surrounding you. Breathe the smoke into your body, letting it pool in your lungs and belly. On the exhale, see it flowing out of you and into your child. This is easiest at first if you hold your baby in your arms, but soon you will be able to do it when just touching your child. Eventually, you'll be able to stand out of sight and accomplish your goal.

But you have to do more than just will your baby to comply. You are projecting your own energy into your child; you must feel that energy yourself. If you're hoping to send blue calming energy, you must feel that calm yourself. If not, you're not projecting what you think you're projecting. Focus on breathing and imbuing your child with the sensations that are in his best interest.

When deciding what color to project, think about what your child needs. Does he need to be calm in order to get to sleep? Try blue. Does he need help figuring out how to feed himself with a spoon? Yellow works here. Is tolerance something he needs? Indigo is perfect. Whatever color you choose, make sure it's something *he* needs, not something *you* desire. Just because you wish he'd go to sleep doesn't mean he *needs* to sleep. Maybe he'll sleep later. If, however, you have a child that simply can't sleep (like my little Falcon), then blue might be just what he needs. Focus on his needs. That's what being a parent is all about.

This method of helping your baby does more than just teach him to calm down or solve problems. Over time, it will teach his subconscious that his feelings and reactions are under his control. He has the power to change how he reacts to the world. This is an empowering thing, even for adults, so teaching it to your child can only help in the long run. This lesson takes time to learn, so you'll need patience, but with time and concentration, your baby will learn self-control and you'll have a stronger bond with your child as they grow into adolescence and eventually adulthood.

Babies are not just smaller people. They function differently than we do. Since they don't use the left side of their brain as often as adults, you won't be able to reason with your baby. You cannot say, "Look, kid, I know you're uncomfortable, but screaming isn't helping." It simply won't compute. We, adults, are the ones with the ability to reason and problem solve. We are the ones who have the ability to meet the needs of our children. And it is our responsibility to do so using whatever tools we have available. One of the greatest tools we have is our own energy, our own aura.

Conclusion

Babies need unconditional love and acceptance. They need us to meet their needs when those needs are expressed. They need to know they can trust Mommy and Daddy to always be there. It's important to remember that your baby is experiencing perhaps the most powerful change any of us will ever have to go through—the transition from the warm and welcoming environment of the womb to the cold and highly individual world we all inhabit. This is a difficult transition, and it's on us to be as gentle and accommodating as possible.

I'm not saying you should just accept being awake all night or feeding constantly. Schedules and routines are good, both for us and for our children. But there is a difference between using all our resources, including our aura, to gently change a baby's natural schedule and forcing him to adhere to something that feels foreign and unnatural to him. The fact that it's neither foreign nor unnatural means nothing, not at the beginning.

You know what else is meaningless? What we think about it. It doesn't matter if you think he doesn't need you. It doesn't matter if your doctor thinks he doesn't need you. It doesn't even matter if he actually doesn't need you. *He* thinks he does. His perception is your reality, at least for most of the first year. The trick is to realize he doesn't necessarily need your body. He simply needs *you*, and you are more than a bag of flesh and bones. Many times your own aura can be used to satisfy his needs. Take advantage of this.

About the Author

Aislin is of Irish, Danish, English, and Romany (Gypsy) descent. Raised on the Canadian prairies, she spent most of her formative years with her maternal grandfather, following him into his garden and through the woods. He introduced her to the magick of nature. It is the magick of her childhood that has the greatest influence on her today.

Aislin is considered a local expert on paganism, the occult, and astrology. She also teaches some local classes on these topics, though The Winnipeg Pagan Teaching Circle. She has been a Wiccan High Priestess since 2000, and has always made an effort to educate seekers when they ask. She founded The Order of the Sacred Star, a group that specializes in educating Pagans of all kinds as well as any other interested parties. Her own children, both boys, are quickly learning the ways of Wicca and seem to embrace nature's magick with vigor. She is also a professional astrologer and Tarot reader, serving her local community in this capacity as frequently as required.

As a writer, Aislin is the author of *Tarot Deciphered: Understanding and Using the Tarot*, which has become a handbook for those new to the Tarot and its uses. She is also the author of the entire *Ash-*

ling Wicca Series, which is the first series of books to publish anything about Ashling Wicca and its teachings.

If you're interested in discovering more about Aislin and her work, connect with her through her blog: http://theorderofthesacredstar.blogspot.com/

www.ingramcontent.com/pod-product-compliance
Lightning Source LLC
Chambersburg PA
CBHW071257140726
47996CB00007B/2883